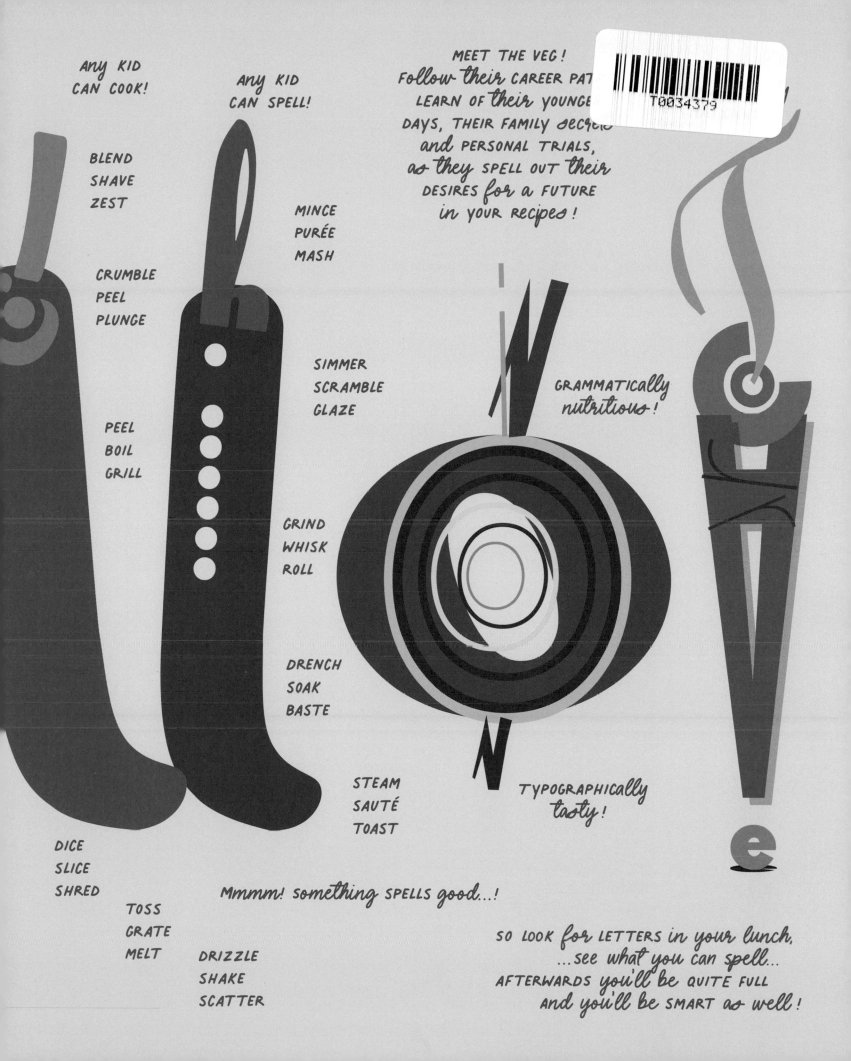

For Lex, Ginger, Bonny and everlasting George.

dedicated to my darling cousin Jo...
...artist, teacher, gardener, cyclist, sister, mother, wife, nanna, friend and inspiration.

Published in 2023 by Melbournestyle Books
155 Clarendon Street, South Melbourne
Victoria 3205, Australia
www.melbournestyle.com.au

A catalogue record for this book is available from
the National Library of Australia
National Library of Australia Cataloguing-in-Publication entry:

Coote, Maree, author, illustrator.

Letters For Lunch! : How to eat the alphabet / Maree Coote, author, illustrator.

ISBN 978-0-6485684-76 (hbk.)

Subjects:
1. Graphic design (Typography) -- Pictorial works -- Juvenile literature.
2. Food -- Pictorial works -- Juvenile literature.
3. Cooking —Pictorial works -- Juvenile literature.
4. Alphabet in art -- Pictorial works -- Juvenile literature.
5. English language -- Alphabet -- Pictorial works -- Juvenile literature.
6. Visual poetry, Australian -- Pictorial works -- Juvenile literature.

Printed in China on wood-free paper

10 9 8 7 6 5 4 3 2 1

MELBOURNESTYLE
BOOKS
www.melbournestyle.com.au

LETTERS FOR LUNCH!

How to eat the alphabet

Find the letters in your lunch, Spell your dinner and your brunch, Right ways, sideways, upside-down, All the letters can be found!

LOOK-AND-FIND • EVERY PICTURE MADE WITH THE LETTERS OF ITS OWN NAME • SPELL-A-PICTURE

LETTER ART

maree coote

Apple

I'll be a **Key Ingredient** one day before I'm rotten,
I'll join a salad in **New York** and never be forgotten.

WALDORF SALAD: apple, lettuce, grapes and MAYONNAISE, celery, WALNUTS, lemon juice... STILL FAMOUS NOWADAYS!

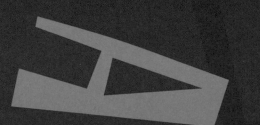

pear

I was tough when I was young... Can't really blame me though,
My entire family tree went pear-shaped long ago.

I want to be a POACHED
DESSERT — a STAR of
FRENCH CUISINE,
and BATHE in WINE and
SUGAR in a FOODIE
MAGAZINE.

orange

Oranges look o-so-sweet but do not be deluded:
Nothing rhymes with orange so they shouldn't be included.

SLICE OFF all my
PITH and SKIN,
EXPOSE my JUICY EDGES,
chop — then TOSS
in COCONUT for SNOWY
ORANGE WEDGES.

Lemon

I try to be my sour best, but often feel betrayed,
I give my sourest juice and zest — but you make lemonade!

LEMON JUICE
put to good use
CAN BRIGHTEN UP A TROUT...
ANY FISH DISH *squished*
with LEMON
BEATS a *fish*
WITHOUT.

AvOCADo

Words of wisdom for the wise: Be like the avocado —
If you have nothing nice to say, stay incommunicado.

THE BEST LIFE
that an AV can have
IS GUACAMOLE DIP...
chilli, GARLIC, lemon,
SALT, tomato,
and a CHIP.

eGg

There's really no point being shy, I know this all too well:
If I wanna be an omelette, I'll have to leave my shell.

I'VE been CRACKED and BROKEN...
BEATEN, FLIPPED and fried,
BUT I stay OPTIMISTIC —
'COS I see the SUNNY SIDE.

WaterMelon

They make us seedless nowadays, which ought to be a crime!
Mother Nature put those seeds in there, one at a time.

FREEZE me into ICY-POPS,
scoop me into SPHERES...
GRILL ME on the BARBECUE
and SERVE with GINGER BEERS.

watermelon

grapes

**Without grapes? No raisins for your Grandma's turkey stuffin',
No sultanas for your muesli, mince pie and /or muffin.**

IF you leave me in THE SUN,
I'LL dry out COMPLETELY...
AND LITTLE KIDS
with LUNCH BOXES will
SCOOP ME UP AND EAT me !

PINEAPPLE

Pineapples make me curious. Who named it? Who designed it? Spell it? Juice it? Crush it! Slush it! Somebody's behind it!

SKEWER me on SHISH-KEBABS INTERSPERSED with PRAWNS, and EAT me in HAWAIIAN SHIRTS on palm tree-shady LAWNS.

Everybody loves me, but the price of fame's extreme!
The whole world wants a piece of me! Usually with ice-cream.

BANANA

IN MY LIFE, I'VE DONE IT ALL—
BEEN FROZEN, grilled AND FRIED...
BAKED, CAKED, SMOOTHIED,
CURRIED, Chipped,
SPLIT AND EMULSIFIED.
(AND ON OCCASION, DRIED.)

PeAS

We are a lean, green team — we work together as a squad,
Because to make a mouthful, it takes at least a pod.

PEAS for salad,
PEAS for mash,
PEAS for soup
with ham...
just UNFREEZE ME,
quick and
EASY-PEASY,
—There I am!

CARROTS

It's true we grew up in the dirt — a childhood far from sunny,
But we've made friends in recipes with Balsamic and Honey!

WE'RE SPELLABLE,
—THAT'S DOABLE,
WE'RE JUICEABLE
AND CHEWABLE...
CRUNCHABLE
AND DIPPABLE,
ROASTABLE
AND STEWABLE.

ONION

I make everybody cry — been that way for years,
The minute that I open up, everyone's in tears.

SEVEN ONION HALVES,
Face-down in a buttered pan,
COVER US with PASTRY,
bake and FLIP—
...an ONION FLAN!

leek

Every time you leek, it's me who ends up in hot water.
You drop me in it every time! Please sauté me — it's shorter.

MY PLAN'S to be inside a PIE with CHICKEN and a ROUX... (A ROUX is just a FLOUR-BASED SAUCE that ANY COOK can do.)

TOMATO

I've got it made here in the sun. You won't hear me gripin'.
I'll be ketchup, soup or sauce as soon as I can ripen.

My cousin was a ROMA,
OVAL-shaped and CONTINENTAL,
They PICKLED HIM when he was GREEN
and he went CONDIMENTAL!

GaRLiC

Chop me, crush me, squash or press — however you extrude me,
Although I smell, I'll keep you well — as long as you include me.

SOMETIMES YOU AVOID ME —
I'VE HEARD THE TALK ABOUT ME.
SURE I'M CRUSHED, BUT I KNOW DINNER'S
NOT THE SAME WITHOUT ME.

I DIP my STALKS in HUMMUS, in YOGHURT, and in CHEESE... sometimes I DIP in TSATSIKI right up to my KNEES!

CELERY

A celery stalk tops any fork — no cutlery can beat it.
This crunchy scoop will never droop,
and when you're done, you eat it!

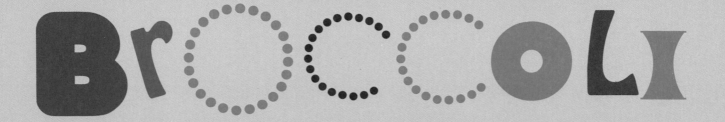

Broccoli

You'll see when you spell broccoli, with all its O's and C's,
That you can't eat the forest before you eat the trees.

I TRY to be UNIQUE —
INVENTING DISHES just for you,
BUT MY COUSIN BROCCOLINI
COPIES EVERYTHING I do !

MUSHROOM

**My parents kept me in the dark, I grew up underground.
Even now I'm grown, I still don't know my way around.**

CORN

**Corn for syrup, flakes and flour, tortillas and polenta...
But best of all is pop-corn! (Our thanks to the inventor.)**

800 kernels on each COB?
APPROXIMATE but TRUE!
A-MAIZE yourself next time
and SIMPLY COUNT
before you chew.

EGGPLANT

'Eggplant', 'Brinjal', 'Aubergine'... 'Nasu' in Japanese,
As long as you invite me, you can call me what you please.

SLICE me thick and GRILL me, ADD fresh TOMATO sauce, then MELTED BOCCONCINI cheese: ...the ULTIMATE FIRST COURSE.

chilli

When you cook with chilli, never <u>ever</u> touch your eyes!
(To those who spell with just one 'L', the same advice applies.)

Jalapeño, habanero, chipotle and bell...
my family can be DANGEROUS—
it pays to KNOW us well.

pepper

Check your pepper: round and sweet? Or long and thin and hot?
Some people's tongues can handle heat, but other's tongues cannot.

I've been SLICED and DICED and STUFFED,
CHAR-GRILLED SO they could PEEL ME,
NO matter WHAT they do to me,
I'LL NEVER TALK— you feel me?

LETTUCE

**Iceberg lettuces are round, that's how it always was.
(Others like Romaine are not. Why's that? Just Cos.)**

These LETTERS will SPELL *lettuce* LEAVES AS NEATLY AS can be. (...REAL LETTUCES have *lots* more *leaves*... I counted THIRTY-THREE!)

Cucumber

'As cool as a cucumber'— that's what they think of me.
The truth is I get butterflies before each recipe.

IF PEOPLE WHO EAT ONLY VEG
ARE LABELLED 'VEGETARIAN'
WOULD VEGIES WHO EAT PEOPLE
BECOME 'HUMANITARIAN'?

BeetRoot

I want to work with famous chefs, I've always been ambitious.
I'm willing to do anything to make myself delicious.

(WELL — NOT REALLY *anything*, LIKE, I WON'T DO THE DISHES.)

CALL ME BEETROOT, CALL ME BEET,
— in SALAD I *taste* BETTER
WITH ROSEMARY and LEMON JUICE,
PEPPER, SALT and FETTA.

RADiSH

Why am I called 'radish'? Is it 'reddish' that they mean?
I see myself as 'pinkish', with bits of white and green.

THE BEST TIME
I HAVE EVER HAD?
BEST SALAD I'VE BEEN IN?
LAST SUMMER...
WITH A FENNEL...
WE WERE BOTH SLICED
VERY THIN.

Pumpkin

I'm a vegie legend, Halloween's my big night out!
I really am the only veg who knows what fame's about.

WHICH RECIPE'S MY FAVOURITE?
I like RAVIOLI BEST...
INSIDE those PASTA PILLOWS
I can finally have a REST.

ZUCCHINI

A pumpkin is a type of squash, and so is a zucchini.
Pumpkins can grow super large. Zucchinis? Teeny-weeny...

...sometimes IN-BETWEENY,
CAN be OLIVE-GREENY,
MAKES vegetable LINGUINI—
A 'NOODLE' THAT'S not PASTA,
SO iT won't STRETCH
your BIKINI.

POTATO

Fried in butter, fried in oil — in fat, or lard, or ghee...
There is no greater calling than The Chip for spuds like me.

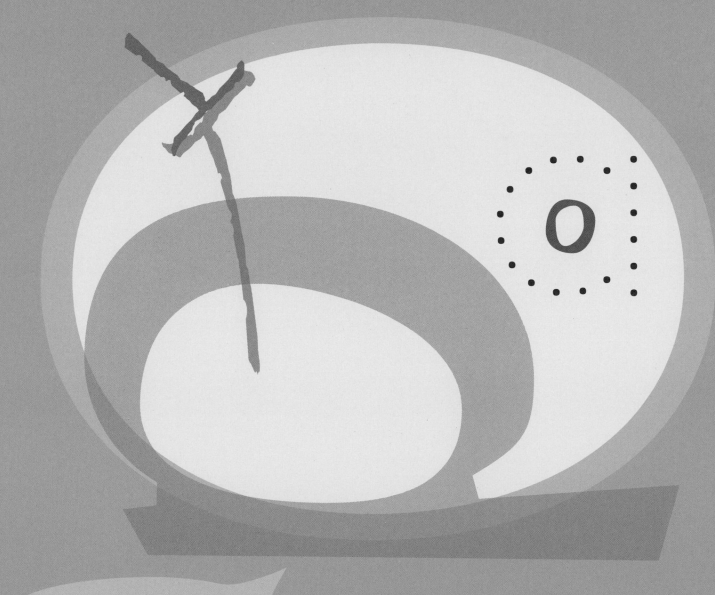

CALL ME DIRTY, UGLY, CHEAP...
JUDGE ME, MOCK ME, DOUBT ME.
FACT IS, there's NOT ONE OF YOU
who'd want to EAT WITHOUT ME.

CLEVER KIDS TEACHERS NOTES:

ABOUT THIS BOOK & LETTER ART

Every picture in this book is made with the letters that spell its name. Each page has a letter 'key' which shows the exact letters and fonts that have been used to create each image. Find these letters in the image, and try Letter Art for yourself!

ABOUT TYPOGRAPHY

A 'font' is a design for a set of letters of the alphabet.

A serif font has letters with little 'feet': A A sans-serif font has letters without little 'feet': A

These are examples of font categories: CAPITAL lower case **Bold** *ITALIC* *script*

FUN FOODIE FACTS

'Recipe' comes from the ancient word for 'receipt'; something received or taken.

The Waldorf Salad was invented in 1896 for a charity ball at the Waldorf Astoria Hotel in New York by Oscar Tschirky, the 'mâitre d'hotel' (master of the house).

Pear-shaped is a phrase used to describe things that go wrong. It is attributed to potters' and glass-blowers' mistakes and misshapen vases and bowls, and also to pilots' wonky attempts at making perfect circular loop-the-loops in mid-air.

Zest is the name we give to finely grated orange/lemon/lime (citrus) peel.

Balsamic vinegar is a rich, syrupy vinegar that has been aged and concentrated.

The Watermelon pip-spitting world record is 75ft 2 inches (22.91m), recorded in 1995 in De Leon, Texas, USA by Jason Schayot. (Guinessworldrecords.com)

A roux is a white sauce. Also called **bechamel**, it is used for lots of dishes from lasagne to chicken pies. Method: Mix 2 tbsp flour and 2 tbsp butter to a paste and slowly add 1 cup milk over a low heat, blending all the time to avoid any lumps. Stop when it's thick and creamy. You can stir in grated cheese for a yummy cheese sauce.

Condiments are sauces, chutneys, salsas, sambals, relishes, pickles, pestos and all kinds of preserved fruits and veg. You can preserve in salt, sugar, vinegar, alcohol, oil or by drying. You can do this when the produce is green or fully-ripened.

Hummus is a dip made of blended chickpeas, tahini, garlic, lemon juice and salt.

Tsatsiki is yoghurt blended with dill, cucumber, garlic, lemon and salt.

'Teppanyaki' is a Japanese word meaning 'teppan' (iron grill plate) + 'yaki' (cooking).

Garlic is a natural antibiotic, antiseptic, antifungal, and can even help de-worm your dog! Garlic can keep you healthy, as it helps the immune system to fight off germs.

Mushrooms are the above-ground fruit of fungi. They come from the powerful, living mycelial network, a hidden underground structure that is often ancient and gigantic. When conditions are right, the fruiting body (mushroom) appears. Poisonous toadstools are also fungi. The deadliest include the Death Cap, the Funeral Bell and the Fool's Mushroom.

The Pepper family (*Capsicum annum*) includes sweet peppers and hot chillis. A Jalapeño chilli is 2,500 –10,000 Scoville Heat Units (SHU). The hottest thing in the world is the Carolina Reaper chilli, which is 1½ million SHU ! Chilli is spelled with double 'L' (UK,AU) and single 'L' (US).

Fetta is a white, salty, crumbly cheese made from goat's milk.

Iceberg lettuce (originally called Crisphead lettuce), got its nickname from California farmers in the 1920s when it was shipped long distances covered in crushed ice. There are many varieties of lettuce, including **Romaine** (US), which is also known as **Cos** (UK, AU).

'Radish' comes from the ancient Latin word 'radic', meaning root.

Zucchini can be made into spaghetti-like noodles using a spiralizer. These can be eaten raw as a salad, or will cook quickly, tossed in some oil, garlic and pesto.

Lard is melted down and purified pig fat.

Ghee is clarified butter used regularly in Indian cuisine.

CLEVER KIDS TEACHERS' NOTES about
Letter Art, Food, Recipes and Animations are available via
www.cleverkids.net.au & www.melbournestyle.com.au

MELBOURNESTYLE
BOOKS
www.melbournestyle.com.au